MAGIC EYE

A New Bag of Tricks

3D Illusions by Magic Eye Inc.

ISBN-10: 0-8362-0768-8
ISBN-13: 978-0-8362-0768-2

Artists: Tom Baccei, Cheri Smith, Andy Paraskevas, Ron Labbe and Bill Clark (as pictured on page 31, from top to bottom.)

Disclaimer: The information contained in this book is intended to be educational and entertaining and is not for diagnosis, prescription, or treatment of any eye conditions or disease or any health disorder whatsoever. This information should not replace competent optometric or medical care. The author is in no way liable for any use or misuse of this material. Our wish is that further research will help to unlock the mystery of how vision and the brain work.

ATTENTION: SCHOOLS AND BUSINESSES

Magic Eye® images are available for educational, business, or sales promotional use. For information, please contact:

Magic Eye Inc., P.O. Box 1986, Provincetown, MA 02657
Tel: 508-487-8484 Email: 3d@magiceye.com

www.magiceye.com

Andrews McMeel books are available at quantity discounts with bulk purchase for educational, business, or sales promotional use. For information, please write to:

Special Sales Department, Andrews McMeel Publishing, LLC, 4520 Main Street, Kansas City, MO 64111.

INTRODUCTION

Magic Eye Books

Welcome to the magical world of Magic Eye®! Magic Eye 3D illusions will challenge and entertain you. Embedded within each Magic Eye image is an enchanting 3D hidden object or scene that materializes before your eyes. Creating a Magic Eye image is a combination of advanced technology and artistic ability. Magic Eye uses its own patented algorithm. The result is a genuine Magic Eye® image.

When Magic Eye books were first published in the 1990's, the response was as amazing as the 3D images emerging from their colorful backgrounds. Viewers could not get these best-selling books fast enough. In fact, *Magic Eye I*, *II*, and *III* appeared on the *New York Times* Bestseller List for a combined 73 weeks. More than 20 million copies of Magic Eye books have been sold in more than 25 languages.

In addition to breaking best-seller list records worldwide, Magic Eye products have received many prestigious awards. One particularly outstanding award was presented to Magic Eye in Germany in 1995; more copies of *Magic Eye: A New Way of Looking at the World* were sold than any other book in German publishing history.

Magic Eye: A New Bag of Tricks is the 17th Magic Eye book to be published.

Viewing Magic Eye Images

While Magic Eye images were originally appreciated for their entertainment value, more and more people are now becoming aware of the health benefits of viewing Magic Eye images. Vision therapists and optometrists worldwide have proven that viewing Magic Eye images are useful for vision therapy. Viewing Magic Eye images may reduce Computer Eye Strain, diminish stress levels, improve overall vision and lengthen attention spans.

In order to view Magic Eye images, you need vision in both eyes. Your eyes need to work together as a focused team. As a result, the left and right sides of your brain are stimulated more while viewing a Magic Eye image. Because of this we have become very popular with anyone studying "whole mind" or "brain synchronization" types of practices including accelerated learning, fast reading, pain management, meditation, yoga and intuition development. These practices focus on inducing the same "mind and body" state you may experience by viewing Magic Eye images.

Three Magic Eye vision improvement books have been published to date, including our 2001 bestseller, *Miru Miru Magu Yokunaru Magic Eye*, by Magic Eye Inc. and Professor Kurita of Tokyo University.

Magic Eye images are also being used as educational tools in schools. Our images "appear" in many science and psychology school textbooks. Thousands of students use Magic Eye as a topic for papers and projects.

Syndication and the Web

Magic Eye syndicated images have been printed in the weekly comics section of numerous newspapers worldwide for over twelve years.

Please visit the Magic Eye website, where over 40,000 visitors a week learn the science and history behind Magic Eye images and techniques. Here you can enter our contests, view numerous Magic Eye images and visit our online store.

I would like to take this opportunity to thank all of you for purchasing our products and for sending us thousands of wonderful letters and emails.

If you are viewing Magic Eye for the first time be sure to follow the viewing instructions on page four, and most importantly, have fun!

Cheri Smith
President & Creative Director
Magic Eye Inc.

www.magiceye.com

VIEWING TECHNIQUES

★   ★

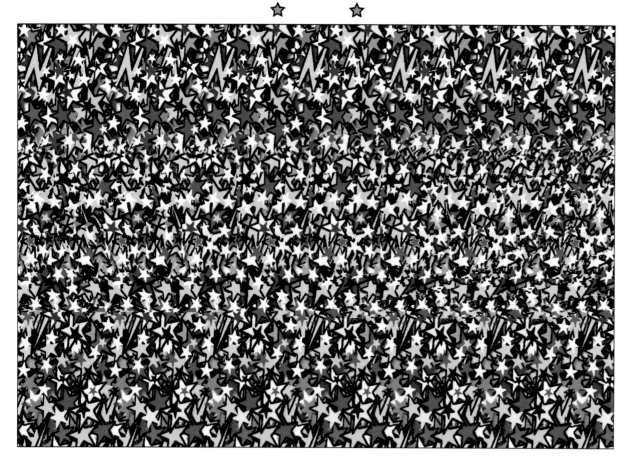

There are two methods for viewing Magic Eye images: diverging your eyes (focusing beyond the image) and converging your eyes (focusing before the image or crossing your eyes). All of the Magic Eye images in this book have been created to be viewed by diverging your eyes.

Instructions #1 for Diverging Your Eyes
(focusing beyond the image)

To reveal the hidden 3D illusion, hold the center of the image *right up to your nose*. It should be blurry. Focus as though you are looking *through* the image into the distance. *Very slowly* move the image away from your face until the two stars above the image turn into three stars. If you see four squares, move the image farther away from your face until you see three stars. If you see one or two stars, start over!

When you *clearly see three stars*, hold the page still, and the hidden image will slowly appear. Once you perceive the hidden image and depth, you can look around the entire 3D image. The longer you look, the clearer it becomes. The farther away you hold the page, the deeper it becomes.

Instructions #2 for Diverging Your Eyes
(focusing beyond the image)

To reveal the hidden 3D illusion, hold the center of this image *right up to your nose*. It should be blurry. Focus as though you are looking *through* the image into the distance. *Very slowly* move the image away from your face until you begin to perceive depth. Now hold the page still and the hidden image will slowly appear.

Magic Eye "Floaters"

Magic Eye "Floaters" are another type of Magic Eye 3D illusion. "Floaters" can first be viewed in 2D, then, by using the standard Magic Eye viewing techniques, "Floaters" will appear to float in 3D space. Floaters and Magic Eye hidden illusions may be combined. (See page 9).

Additional Viewing Information

Discipline is needed when a Magic Eye 3D illusion starts to "come in" because at that moment you will instinctively try to look at the page rather than looking through it, or before it. If you "lose it," start again.

If you converge your eyes (focus before the image or cross your eyes) and view an image created for diverging your eyes, the depth information comes out backward, and vice versa! This means if we intend to show an airplane flying in front of a cloud, if you converge your eyes you will see an airplane-shaped hole cut into the cloud! Another common occurrence is to diverge or converge your eyes twice as far as is needed to see the hidden image, as for example when you see four squares above the image instead of three. In this case, you will see a scrambled version of the intended hidden image.

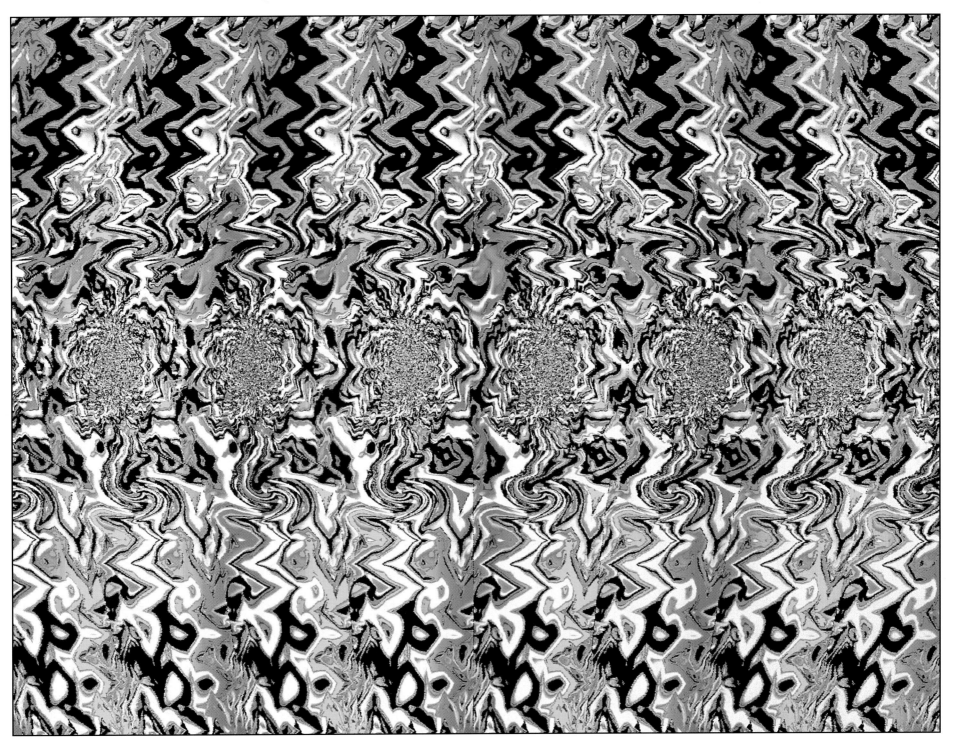

N.E. Way You Look

King of the Cave

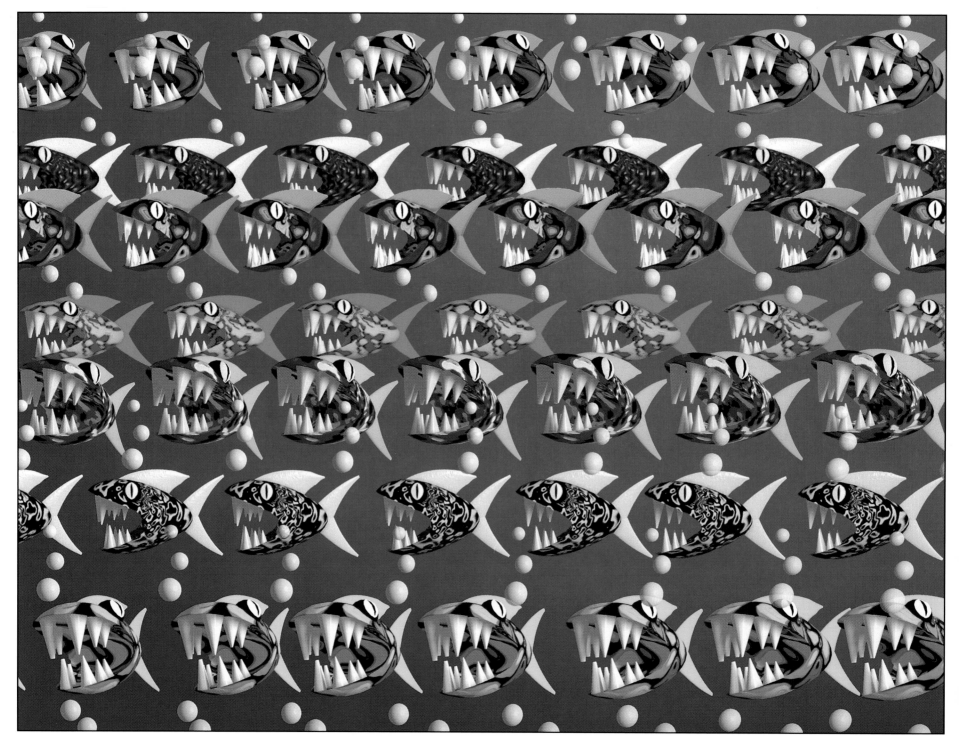

Killer Piranha

Ocean Light

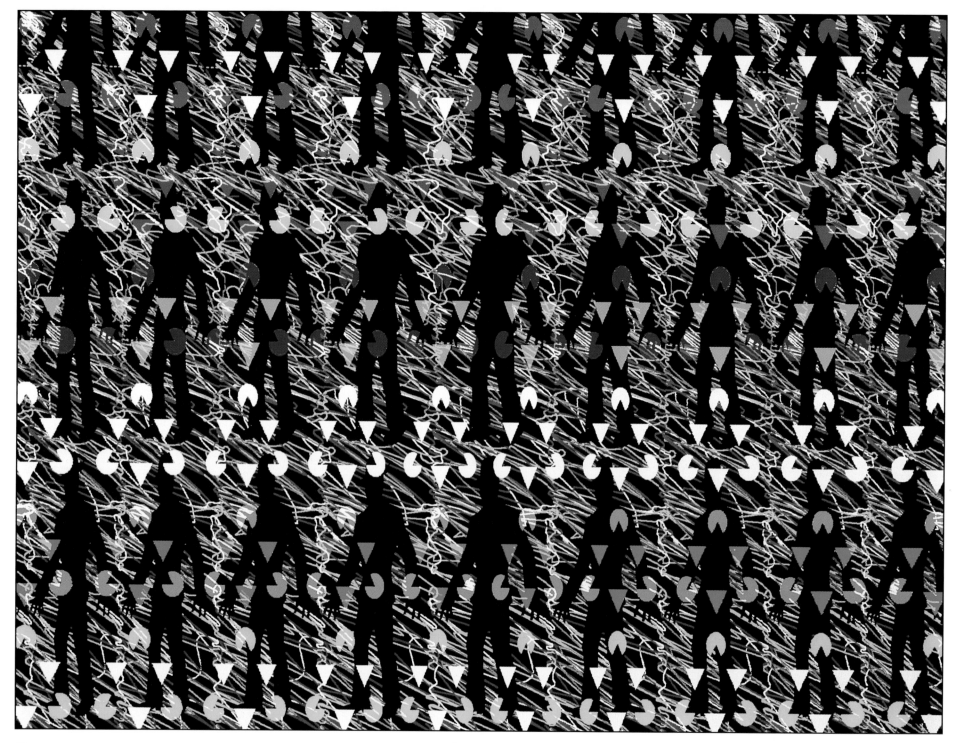

The Suit Guy

Rubies May Tricks

Flower Shower

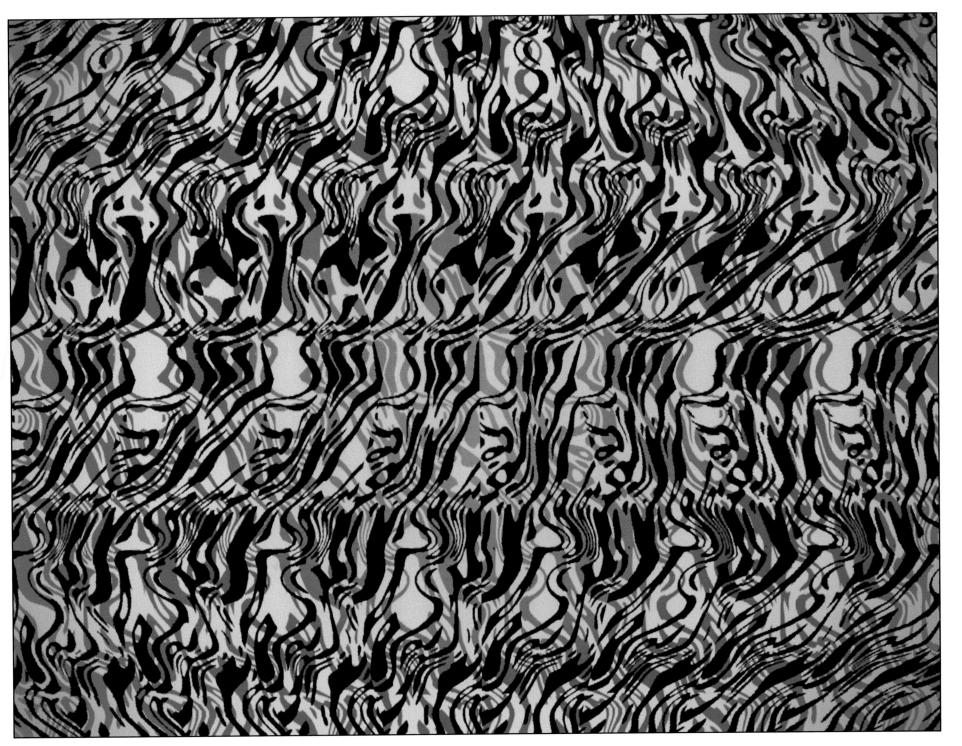

Land of Myths

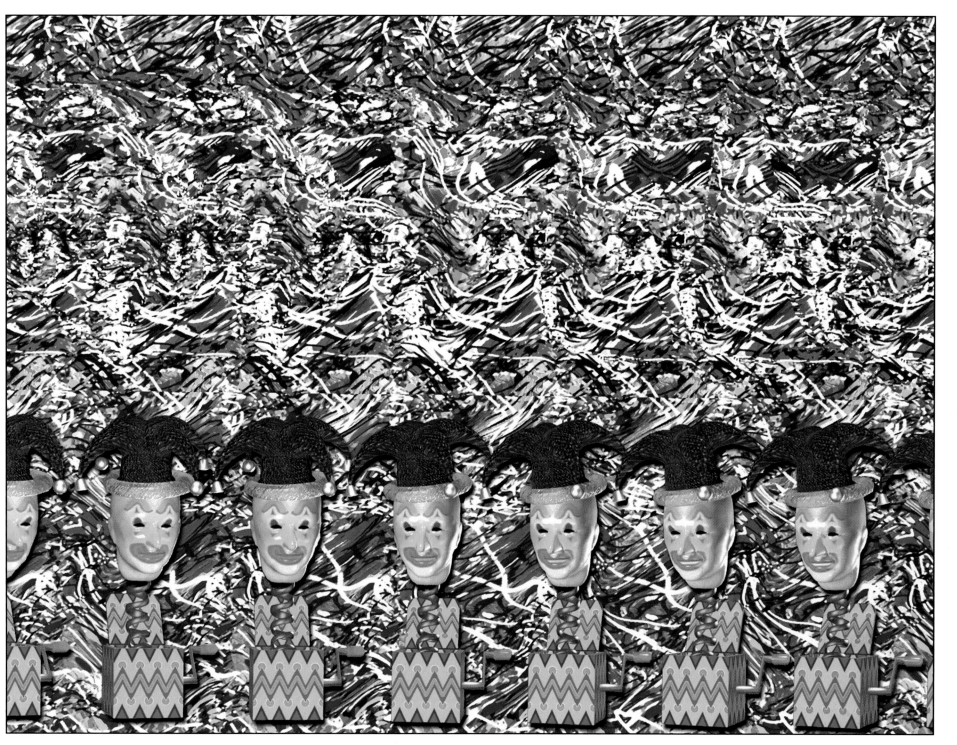

Ramp Page

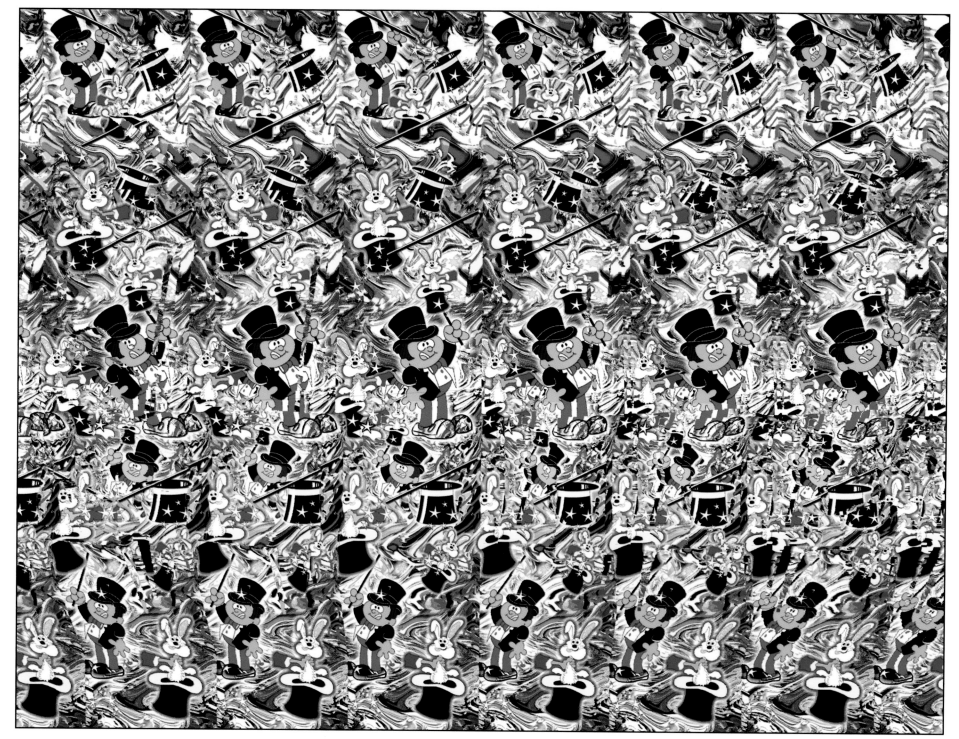

Magic Trick

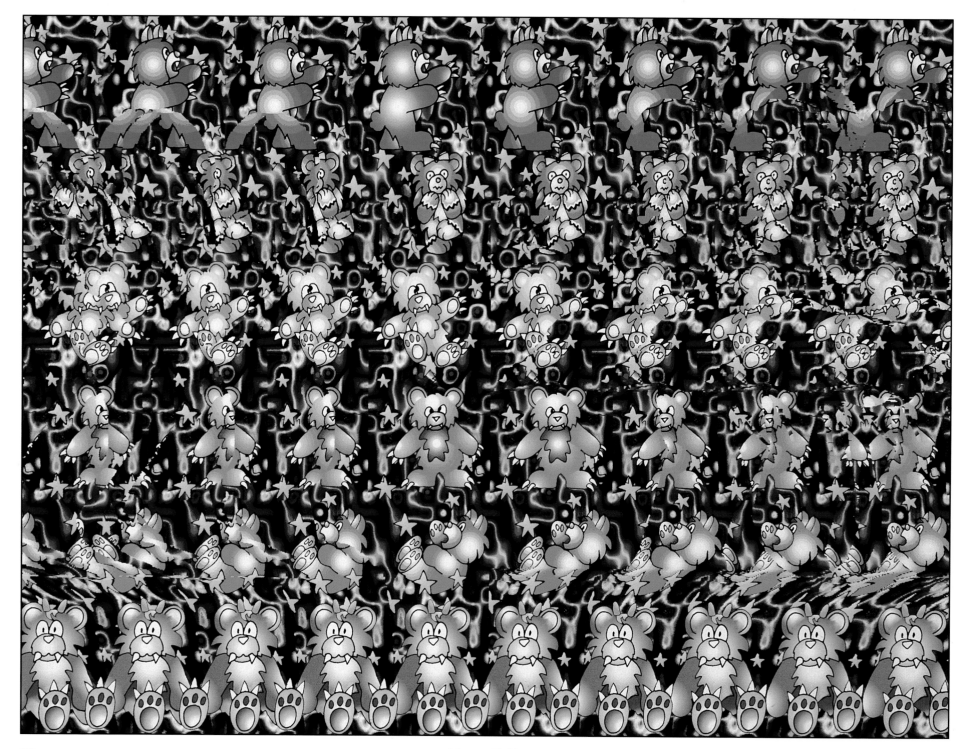

Mutant Teddy

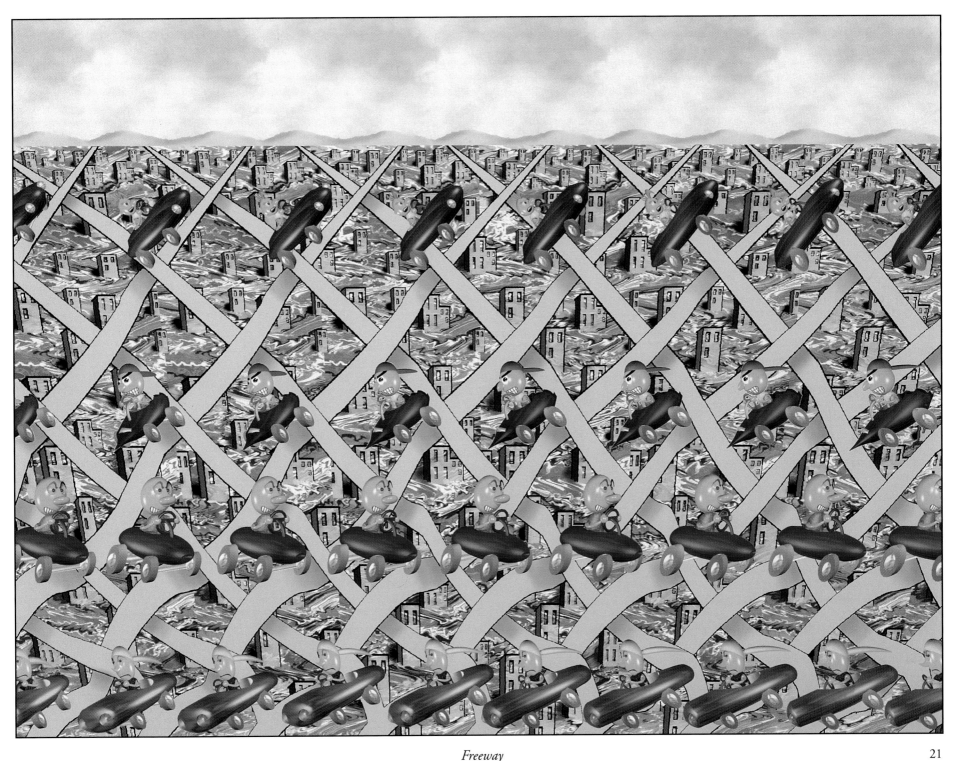

Freeway

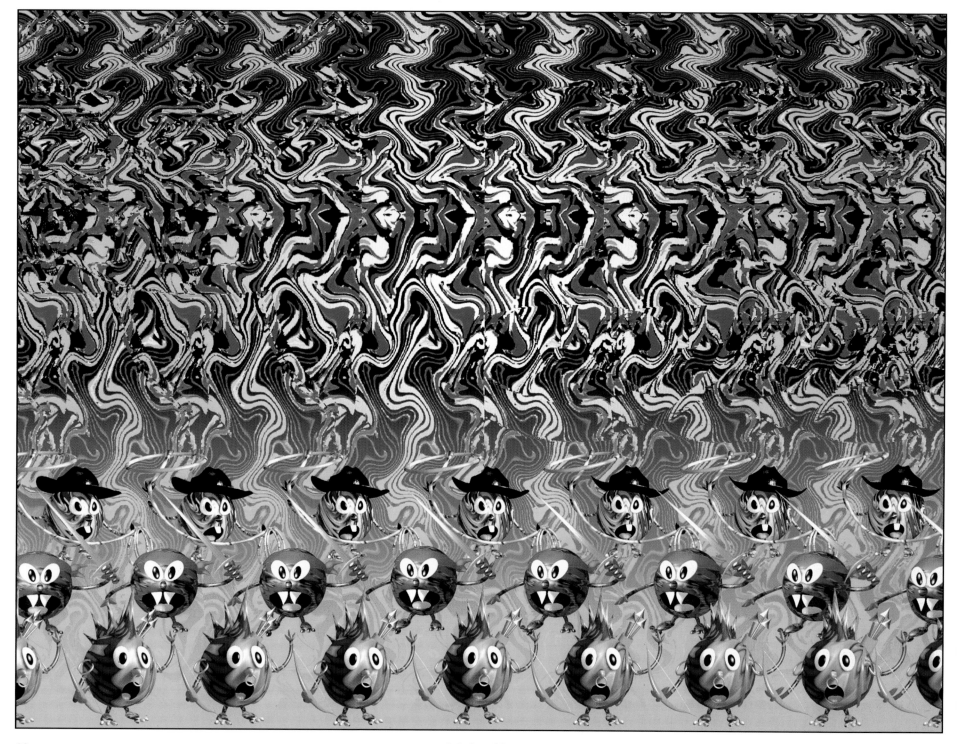

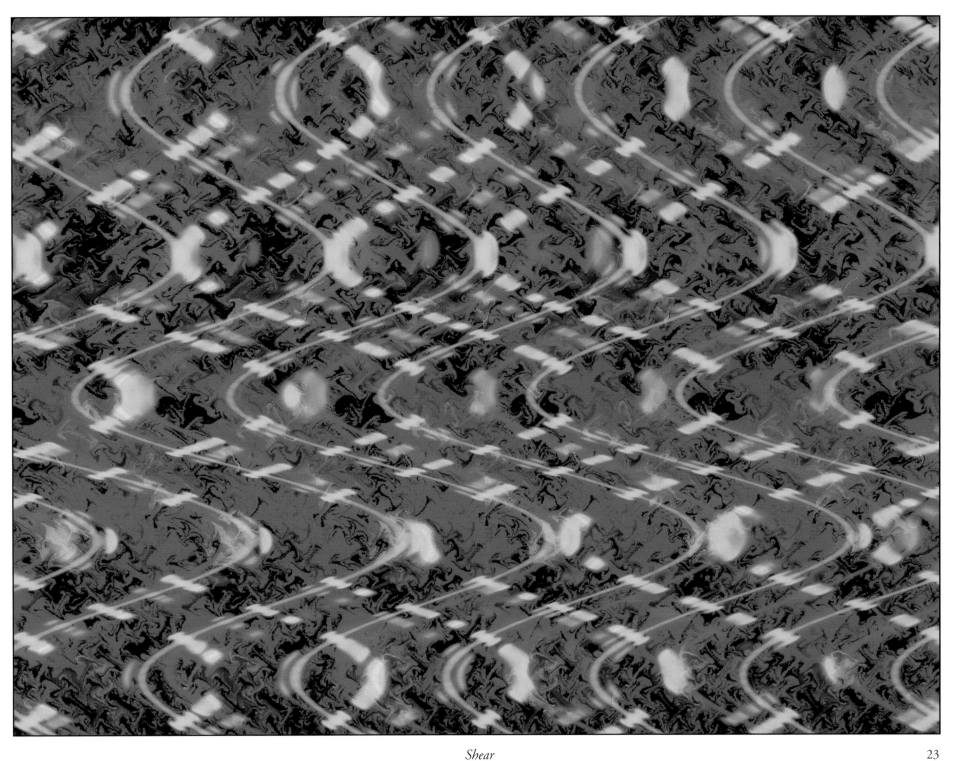

Shear

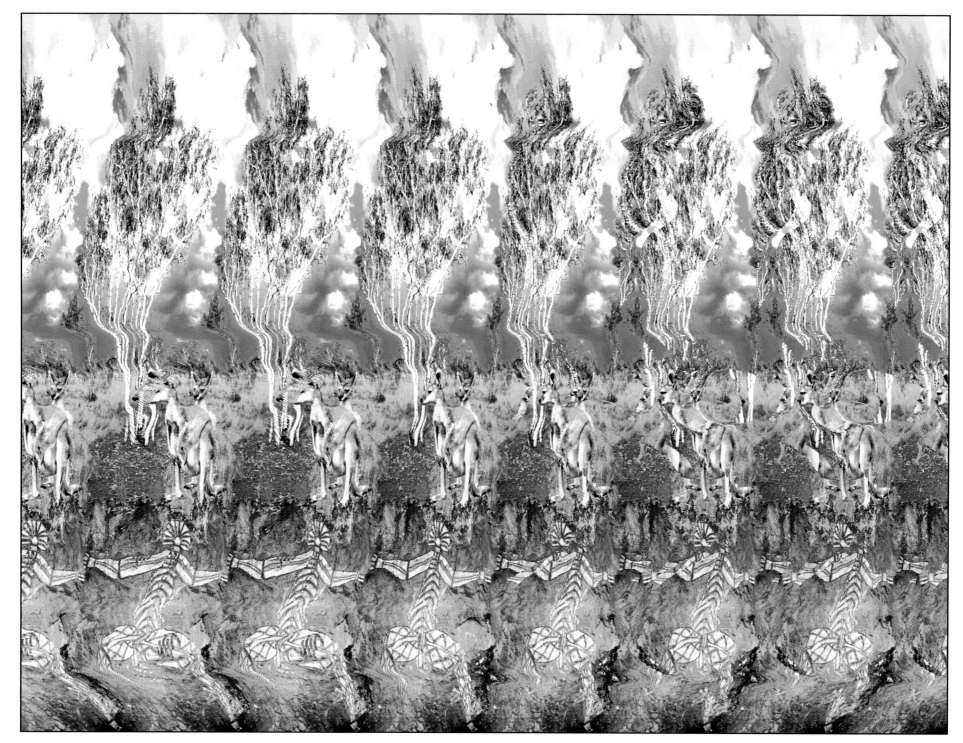

The Outback

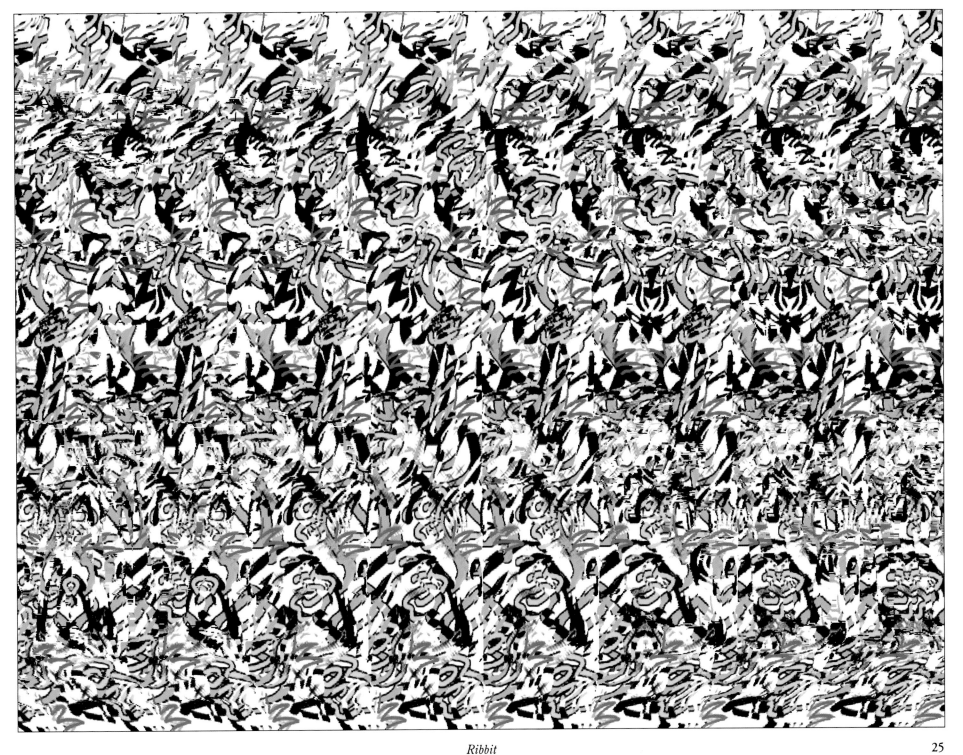

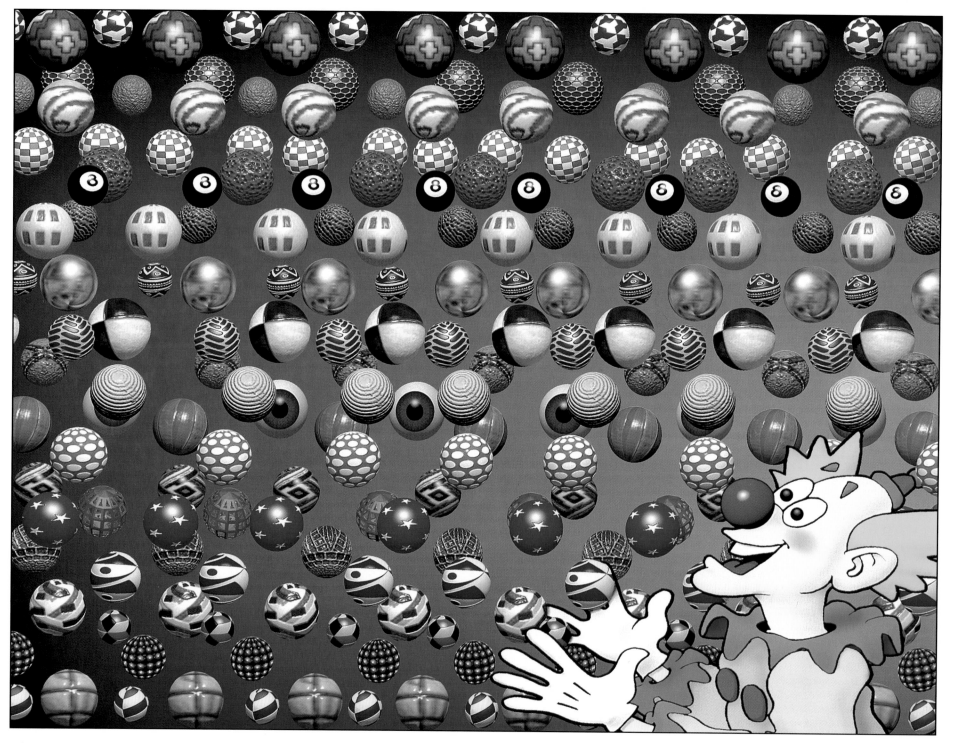

Air Balls

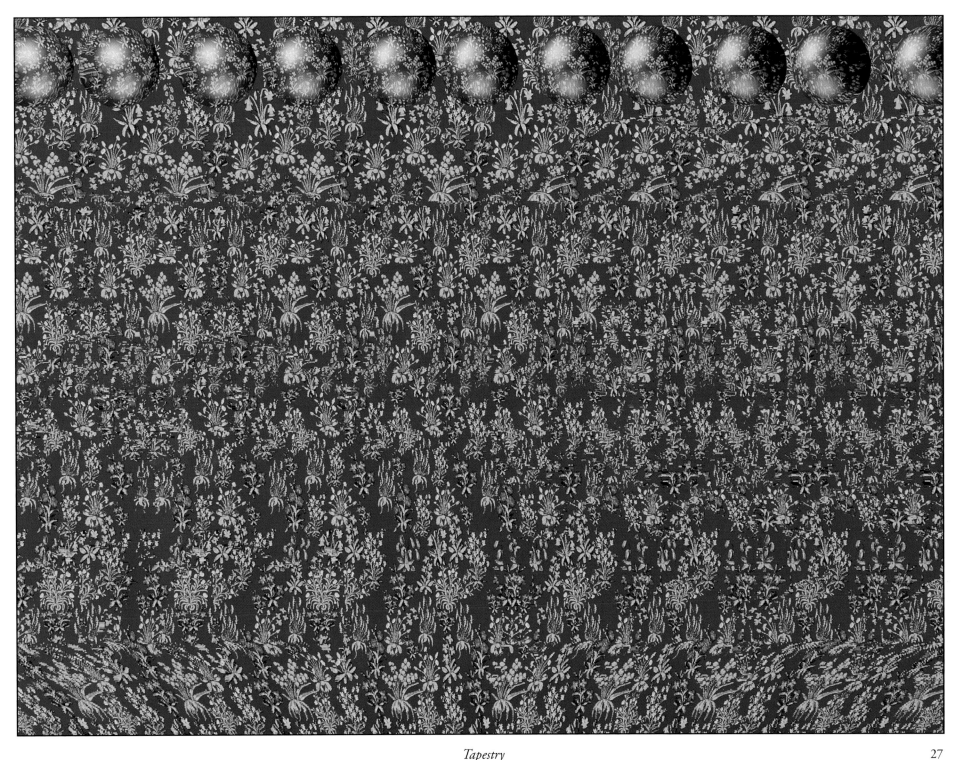

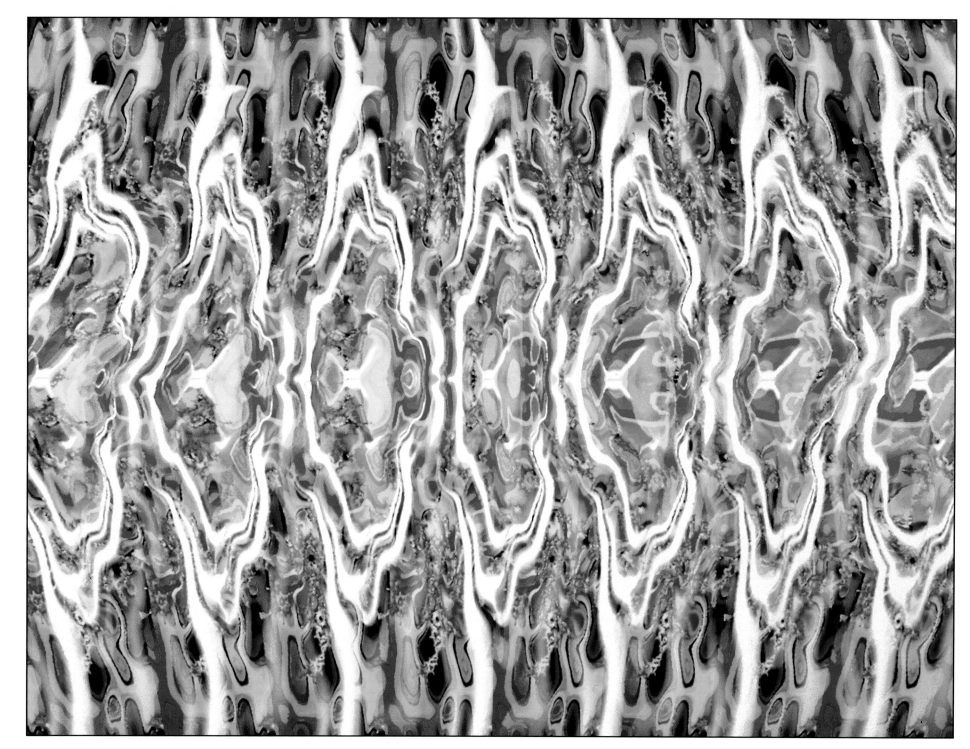

Perception Escapes Me

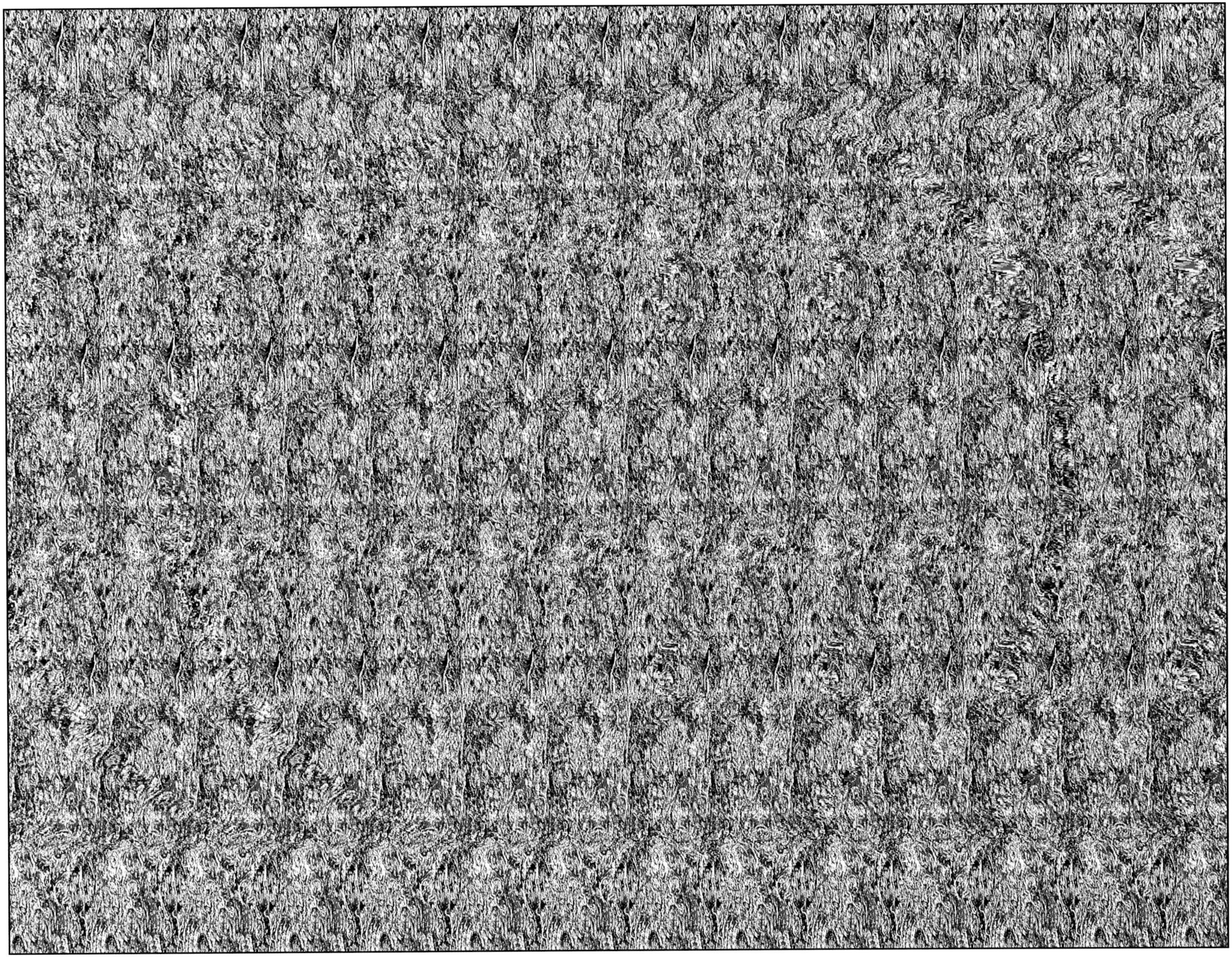

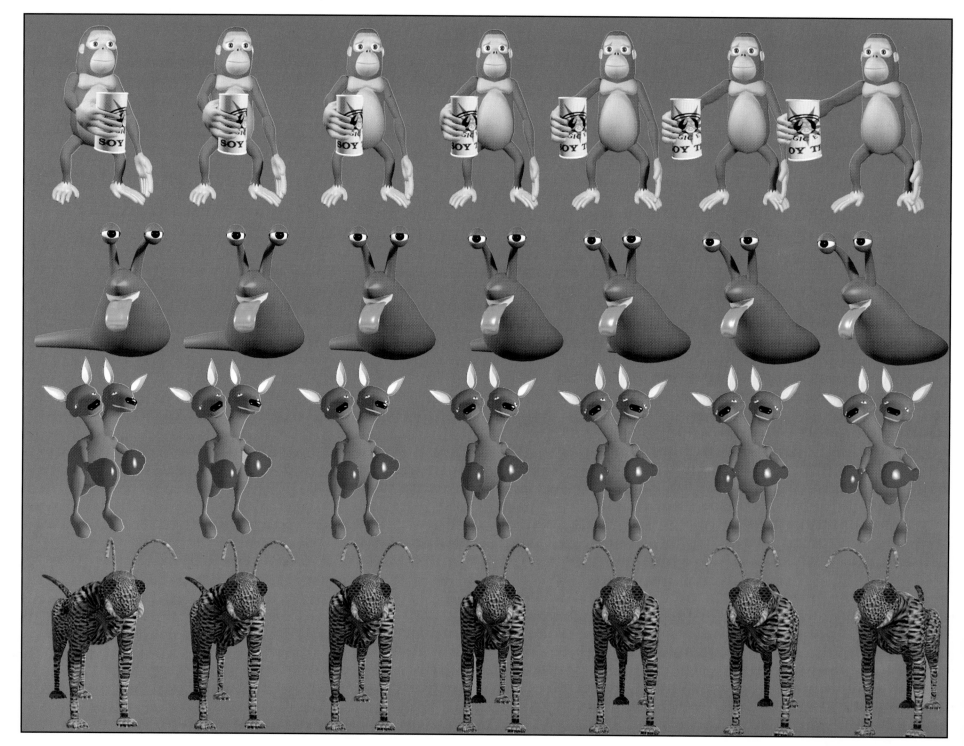

N.E. Mals

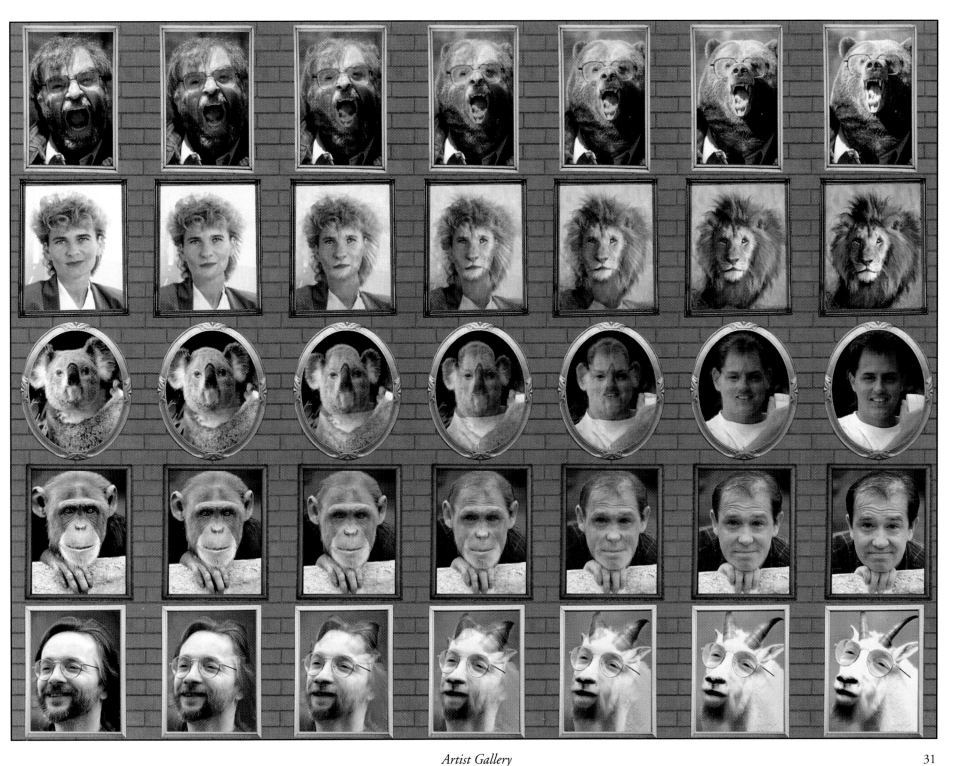

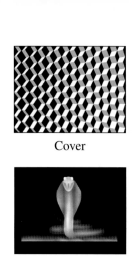

Cover

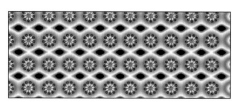

Front End Pages

Viewing Techniques

Page 5 Color Blind

Page 6 N.E. Way You Look

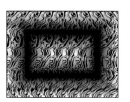

Page 7 King of the Cave

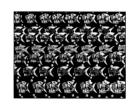

Page 8 Killer Piranha

Page 9 Ocean Light

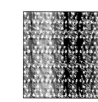

Page 10 The Suit Guy

Page 11 Rubies May Tricks

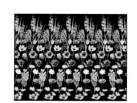

Page 12 Flower Shower

Page 13 Inside Out

Page 14 Land of Myths

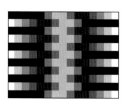

Page 15 What's in the Box?

Page 16 Ramp Page

Page 17 Twister

Page 18 Magic Trick

Page 19 Troo Luv

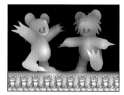

Page 20 Mutant Teddy

Page 21 Freeway

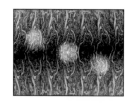

Page 22 Madmarbles

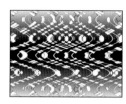

Page 23 Shear

Page 24 The Outback

Page 25 Ribbit

Page 26 Air Balls

Page 27 Tapestry

Page 28 Perception

Page 29 Second Convergence

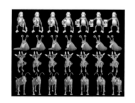

Page 30 N.E. Mals

Page 31 Artist Gallery

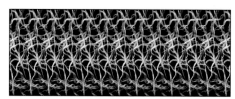

Back End Pages

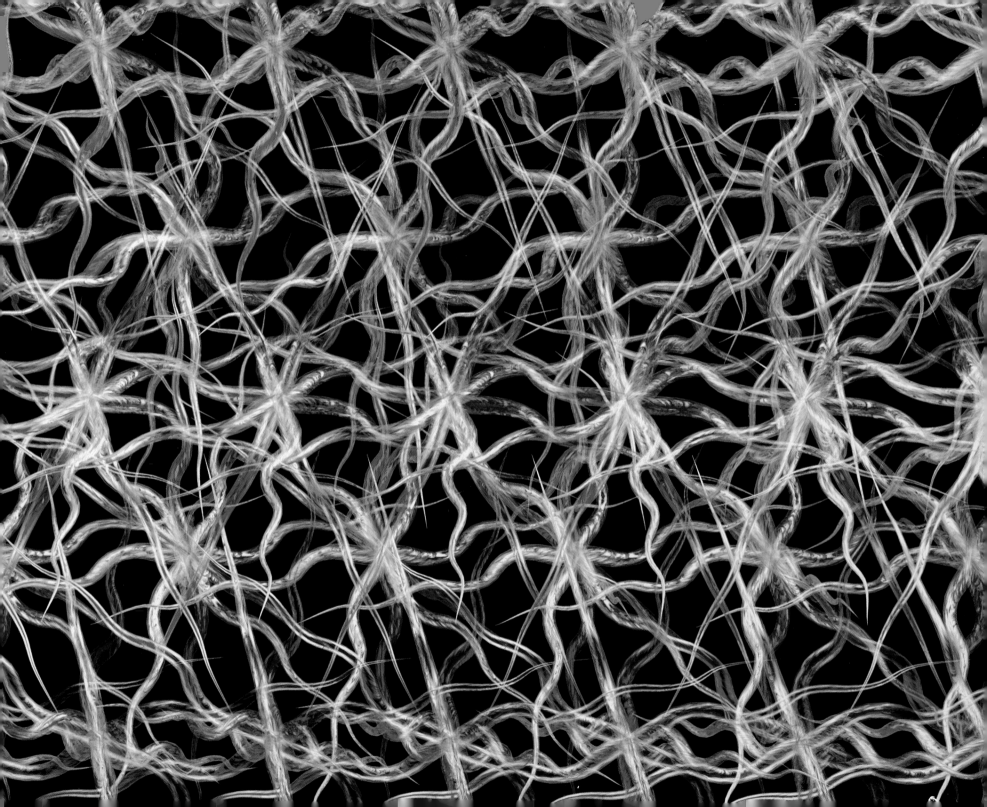